William Kingsland

The Esoteric Basis of Christianity, or, Theosophy and Christian

Doctrine

A Paper read before the Blavatsky Lodge of the Theosophical Society

William Kingsland

The Esoteric Basis of Christianity, or, Theosophy and Christian Doctrine
A Paper read before the Blavatsky Lodge of the Theosophical Society

ISBN/EAN: 9783743394797

Manufactured in Europe, USA, Canada, Australia, Japa

Cover: Foto ©Lupo / pixelio.de

Manufactured and distributed by brebook publishing software
(www.brebook.com)

William Kingsland

The Esoteric Basis of Christianity, or, Theosophy and Christian

Doctrine

The Esoteric Basis of Christianity

OR

Theosophy and Christian Doctrine.

A Paper read before the Blavatsky Lodge of the Theosophical Society

BY

Wm. KINGSLAND, F.T.S.

AUTHOR OF "THE HIGHER SCIENCE," "CONCEPTS OF EVOLUTION AND RELIGION," "THEOSOPHY AND ORTHODOXY," ETC.

———※———

" Wisdom in a Mystery, even the Wisdom that hath been hidden."
ST. PAUL.

———⇒φ⇐———

𝕷𝖔𝖓𝖉𝖔𝖓:

Theosophical Publishing Society, 7, Duke Street, Adelphi, W.C.

THE PATH, 132, NASSAU STREET, NEW YORK, U.S.A.

1891.

London:

WOMEN'S PRINTING SOCIETY, LIMITED,

21B, GREAT COLLEGE STREET, WESTMINSTER, S.W.

THE ESOTERIC BASIS OF CHRISTIANITY

OR

THEOSOPHY AND CHRISTIAN DOCTRINE.

A Paper read before the Blavatsky Lodge of the Theosophica Society,

By Wm. KINGSLAND, F.T.S.

"Wisdom in a Mystery, even the Wisdom that hath been hidden."—St Paul

THEOSOPHY claims to be the truth underlying all religions in their *exoteric* or popular form; and it claims this in virtue of its being a presentation or interpretation of a very ancient system known as the *Secret Doctrine*, or ancient *Wisdom Religion*. The world has never been without its *Initiates*, who have preserved the *esoteric* knowledge which has assumed such numerous *exoteric* forms in all ages. This *esoteric* knowledge, however, has always been guarded with the greatest care, and preserved a profound secret, for reasons which have been fully dealt with elsewhere. I need merely instance here the instruction of Jesus to his disciples, not to cast their pearls before swine; and also the statement of St. Paul (I. Cor., iii., 1) that he was only able to feed his converts with milk, not with meat. The "Wisdom in a Mystery" has been reserved, as St. Paul says (I. Cor., ii., 6), for the perfect or full-grown, for those who have attained to *spiritual* manhood: something which is altogether different from, and not coincident with, physical or intellectual manhood.

The particular point however to which I wish to direct your attention, and which is a fundamental one before we can establish any relation between Theosophy and Christian Doctrine, is this: that in the nature of things, in the nature of history, of human progress and development, in the nature of man's capacity for growth, for the expansion of his limited and relative mind and consciousness, in the nature of the universe itself, there is and must be an inner and an outer, an esoteric and an exoteric; an outward form, and an inner meaning; an outward expression, temporary, finite, mutable, an inner *principle*, eternal, unvarying. If there be any *reality* whatever, underlying what we term *phenomena*, the objective changeable world of sense and form, that reality must constitute an inner *mystery*, which is a *mystery* simply on account of our inability to sense and cognise it, owing to our limited faculties. And if there be any *reality* in that growth, development, or evolution, which is the most prominent factor in our experience, that reality consists in our coming into more and more intimate *conscious* relation to this inner principle which underlies phenomena; consists in an apprehension of the noumena; in the casting-off of the temporary illusion of *form*, of that bondage of the senses which causes attachment to form, attachment to the impermanent and temporary, whereby the permanent and eternal is lost sight of; consists, in short, of the development of that faculty which cognises unity in diversity; or in a word consists of—spirituality.

In theosophical language this faculty resides in the fifth principle, or *Manas*, in the immortal spiritual Ego. (See diagram, page 23.) But setting aside specific theosophical doctrines, let us see what relation this principle of an inner spiritual reality and an outer expression in *form*, and of a corresponding evolution or expansion of human consciousness from particulars to universals, bears to the subject before us.

It is well known that the claim which has been made by the Church, from its earliest traditions down to our present day, on behalf of Christian doctrine, has been that of a special divine revelation by a personal God. Beginning with the first chapter of Genesis, and ending with the last verse of Revelation, we are asked to believe that the collection of ancient writings known as the Bible has been specially prepared and inspired by this personal God, as a record of his dealings with, and his will towards, the creatures he originally created. This I believe may be accepted as the fundamental basis of Christian doctrine, the centre round which all the teachings of the Church, whether Protestant or Catholic, has revolved, and from which they cannot get away without breaking up and destroying all that has ever been known historically as *Christianity*. I say specifically that this is the claim made by the *Church*, because it is a fact commonly overlooked, and one indeed of which the majority of professing Christians are ignorant, that what is known as Christianity, in its doctrinal form, in its traditions, and in the selection and compilation of the subject matter of the Bible, is purely ecclesiastical. The Bible in its present form, the creeds, and the rites and ceremonies which go to make up the sum total of what is known historically as Christianity, were compiled by the early Church authorities from miscellaneous sources. This, however, is a matter of literary and historical data into which I cannot enter now; but I wish it to be understood that in speaking of Christianity and Christian doctrine I am dealing at present with its ecclesiastical and historical forms, and not with the personality or teachings of its supposed founder.

We have then this fundamental idea of Christianity as a revelation of the personal relationship between a creative God, and the creatures he created; and upon this basis is built up the doctrinal superstructure with which we are all familiar in its many variations and modifications.

Now the question which we have before us, in connection with the principle of expansion of the human mind which I have already laid down, is simply this:—is there room within the limits of Christian doctrine within that system known as Christianity, for this natural evolution and expansion? Does Christianity give us, as it claims to do, all that is necessary for man to know of his spiritual nature and destiny? We may even narrow the question down, and setting aside all the varied, and often conflicting teachings of the churches, we may confine ourselves to the root idea, and ask whether the relationship of man to a personal creator which Christianity postulates, is a permanent or only a temporary phase in the evolution of the human mind and consciousness.

Let me point out here the great mistake which is made by all religionists and sectarians with regard to what they call the *truth* of their own particular doctrines. A doctrine is simply a formulated statement of a principle: and since the human mind is only capable of dealing with that which is *relative*, is only capable of formulating principles which are relative to its limited and finite consciousness: and since every mind differs in some degree in its powers of observation and intuition : what is called the *truth* of a doctrine is merely a term for its *relativity*, for the relation which it bears to the individual mind at a certain stage of its experience or evolution. Uniformity of doctrine and belief is impossible, except in a world where every individual is at the same level or point of evolution, and all progressing, or it may be retrogressing, at the same rate.

The mistake which is made by the individual, the sect, or the Church, (and Theosophists need to be warned against this quite as much as others) is in supposing that what is true to them, or true of their own experience, must be true for all the rest of humanity. It is this constant tendency to individualize and restrict, which gives rise to dogmatism, hatred, bigotry, and all the uncharitableness of sectarian religion.

But, I can hear some say, if *truth* be thus merely relative, what test or assurance have we of anything? None whatever, I reply, save the assurance of your own judgment, of your own mind and consciousness. Do not deceive yourselves in this matter, as you value your eternal salvation, as you wish to escape from this fatal illusion of relativity, into the realm of eternal truth. Those who make this fact of man's ignorance the basis of doctrines of revelation and infallibility, are guilty of self-deception and sophistry. The man who asserts his belief in an infallible book, or an infallible church, is exercising his own individual judgment just as much as the man who asserts his right to question both. The final test in each case is the test of individual experience.

But although all that we call *truth* is thus relative, there is one test, one principle, which cannot be ignored, and which must always decide as to the value of truth, must decide as between truth and error. This principle may be defined as that of *universality*. So long as we confine our attention to one set of phenomena, to a limited area of experience, all that is postulated as theory or doctrine may be true in relation to that with which we are dealing. But when other phenomena or experience is brought in as a factor, we must, if it does not harmonize with our previous conclusions, extend our conceptions and doctrines so as to include the new area. The test of truth therefore is its *universality*; it must harmonize all known phenomena, and every factor in human experience; and if we find any set of doctrines dealing merely with a limited portion, and inapplicable to the rest, we have to reject them for wider and deeper principles. Ideas which are absolutely absurd to those who have a wider range of experience, are often "gospel truth" to lesser minds. The distinction between the untutored savage and the member of a civilized community is a very marked one in this respect, but where are we to draw a line, where fix upon a limit, where find the individual who stands at the furthest point of human progress? *We can only draw the line where the possibility of further experience ceases.* And since man is finite, and the universe infinite, the possibility is also infinite. The ideas of the most advanced philosopher of to-day, will one day be regarded as we now regard the primitive ideas of the savage. And if this be not merely possible, but inevitable, as the human race advances: why should there not be those who have already reached that far point of development, who already stand as far removed from the modern scientist or philosopher as the latter does from the savage?

In this vast universe, which appears as one grand field of consciousness, individualized in innumerable manifestations of varying degrees, and ever progressing activity, we can conceive no break in the ever-widening circle. The fundamental axiom of the Unity of the Universe forbids us to conceive of any part or portion, of any manifestation or individualization, which does not share in degree and kind in the universal conscious-ness. There is no single atom of so-called *dead* matter, no single cell or organism, however minute or rudimen-tary, which is not instinct with this universal principle of *consciousness*, which is the basis of all manifestation, phenomena, and sensation. Assuredly it was this idea which inspired our own poet Tennyson to write :—

" Flower in the crannied wall,
I pluck you out of the crannies ;—
Hold you here, root and all, in my hand,
Little flower—but if I could understand
What you are, root and all, and all in all,
I should know what God and man is."

And as we can trace this principle in all stages of evolution, in ever-widening spheres of consciousness up to man, so we are bound to go on with the process, and conceive of individual intelligences of higher, wider, and nobler character, until the whole series is summed up in that absolute consciousness of the whole, which we can postulate and name, as God or otherwise, but of which we can form no conception, and therefore formulate no doctrine.

And this is not merely true as a speculation of the mind, one which has found expression in all ages in various conceptions of superior beings, in Gods, Angels and Archangels, Dhyan Chohans, &c.: but it is claimed as an actual fact that there are those human beings, with no elements of supernaturalism or superstition about them, who stand to-day where the majority of men will only stand after thousands, and it may be millions of years. Why not ? I ask again, where are you going to draw the line at the possibility of further human progress ? And if the gulf is so great to-day between the savage and the philosopher, why should there not be as great a gulf between the philosopher and the adept ? The existence of these Masters of Wisdom is a fact, which all may prove who are not too prejudiced to investigate and form an unbiassed judgment.

And now observe in connection with this relativity of doctrine to the experience of the individual, its application to what has been called *revealed truth*, as distinguished from human discovery. There is no possibility of revelation save in connection with the relative nature and capabilities of the individual mind. " I have yet many things to say unto you, but ye cannot bear them now " (John xvi., 12). Revelation necessarily deals with that which is subjective, with that which is supposed to be beyond the reach of actual experience or observation; and it is just here that we have the special claim of Christianity, that it supplies information which man could not in the nature of things have found out for himself. In Christian dogma the Bible is nothing if not superhuman.

But the whole question is, what is superhuman ? To the savage there is much that would appear superhuman in that which is familiar in the every-day experience of the civilized man. To the average man of to-day, even to the most advanced scientist—and probably more so to him by reason of his one-sidedness —the powers of the adept appear superhuman, and are therefore denied. Much that has at one time been denied as belonging to the category of the *supernatural* is now admitted, as having been brought within the line of the natural. Science denied the facts of mesmerism, but is now compelled to recognise them. It denies the facts of spiritualism, and will not investigate because it has settled beforehand that the phenomena are impossible.

Professor Tyndall says:—"There are men of science who would sell all that they have, and give the proceeds to the poor, for a glimpse of phenomena which are mere trifles to the spiritualist." And yet he will not investigate, although one of the most eminent scientific men of the day, Professor Crookes, has published scientific researches which give something more than the required glimpse. On the other hand Professor Huxley virtually contradicts Professor Tyndall when he says:—"Supposing the phenomena to be genuine, they do not interest me." And so he also will not investigate. These men have made up their minds that there cannot be anything supernatural or superhuman, and they define these as anything which lies outside the range of their own particular experience.

The Christian makes exactly the same mistake in the opposite direction. He has made up his mind that his Bible is superhuman and revealed, and not only so, but that there is no other record in the world which can make a similar claim, or can be compared in any respect with this book ; and starting from this as a first principle he is compelled to reject all other records, religions, and experience as false and mischievous.

Before we can decide then as to the authority of the Bible, as a supposed superhuman record, we must first of all decide as to the limits of the human, as to the line of demarcation between the human and the superhuman, between the natural and the supernatural. And if there be no such line—or rather if the line be relative, not absolute—if the possibility of human development be infinite, as indeed all reason and analogy lead us to conclude ; if further than this we have direct evidence that there are, and always have been, those who are so much in advance of the race that they stand in the position usually assigned to the superhuman : we have offered to us at once a rational solution of the difficulties in connection with the Bible record. Let us glance at a few of these difficulties before presenting more specifically the solution which Theosophy offers.

We may divide these difficulties into two classes : (a)

historical, literary, and critical; (*b*) doctrinal; or briefly: those which relate to facts, and those which relate to doctrine. It is necessary to make this distinction because facts are so often confounded with doctrine in matters of controversy. The facts of the Bible, and the doctrines based thereon, are two totally different things. A fact must underlie a doctrine, it is the basis on which doctrine rests, and if the supposed fact be found to be false, the doctrine must necessarily be false also. In too many cases this is reversed, and fact is made to rest upon doctrine, as in the instances I have educed of the attitude of mind of the scientist and religionist respectively. The position taken up by each of these is, that if the facts and the doctrine do not harmonize, so much the worse for the facts. We must observe, however, that so long as the fact is admitted, or supposed, or stands as a first principle, the doctrine may be relatively true to that fact, although absolutely false. On the other hand a fact may be admitted, but the conclusions drawn from that fact be widely different.

Now we have in the Bible a record which on the face of it appears to be historical; on what grounds are we to decide its validity as history; how are we to decide as to the truth of the statements it puts forward as statements of facts? The common argument is, that it is true because it is the inspired word of God, but that is putting doctrine before fact; and as such a large portion of it is evidently untrue as matter of fact, the doctrine of inspiration becomes a difficult one to accept. Modern apologists endeavour to strike a kind of mean between the old doctrine of literal inspiration, and the idea that the Bible is purely human in its origin. This, however, is merely one of those forced concessions by which the Church is dragged in the rear of advancing thought, which she vainly endeavours to retard.

We have then in the first place the fact of the existence of the Bible, and in the second place the doctrine of the Church with regard to its origin and inspiration. We have in the first place certain statements made in the Bible with regard to supposed facts in history, and in the second place the doctrines of the Church built up upon these statements.

It is no part of my task now to enter into controversy on these matters. What I wish to do is to state the question so that we may see clearly where it is that Theosophy offers a solution of the difficulties which beset the earnest student, and more especially those who are endeavouring to free themselves from the narrow and inconsistent concepts of Christian orthodoxy. Theosophy has much to offer to these enquirers; a great responsibility rests upon Theosophists in connection with the revolution through which so many minds are passing in connection with the elements of the faith in which they have been brought up. There is, I fear, too much tendency on the part of those who have passed through this stage, and reached the goal of freedom, to look with something approaching to contempt upon those who are still unable to enter into that freedom. There is a contempt of intellect, as well as a contempt of wealth; an air of *nouveau riche* in the one as in the other. There is much need that we should bear in mind the injunctions of St. Paul as to our behaviour towards our weaker brethren, those who are not yet freed from the bondage of forms and ceremonies, of custom, prejudice, and early training and bias. While jealously guarding our own freedom, while boldly denouncing those systems which are responsible for the moral and intellectual thraldom of so many of our fellow-creatures: those systems which take advantage of ignorance in order to enslave it by means of superstitious fear; let us be careful lest thereby we cause our weaker brethren to stumble. There is a flagrant and blatant atheism in vogue in some quarters which delights in holding up to ridicule of the grossest form, matters which are sacred to many minds. I do not think any Theosophists can be in sympathy with such. But there are hundreds and thousands to-day, who are questioning the basis of the Christian faith, and are going through a mortal struggle in their efforts to reach that *something* which is dimly perceived to lie

outside and beyond the teachings of the Church. The success of *Robert Elsmere* was due to the skill with which the author portrayed this stage of doubt and questioning through which so many are passing. Some of us have passed through it in a more or less acute form in this incarnation, others have not experienced it now, having passed through it before ; but assuredly at some time or another all must fight and conquer that particular illusion which enslaves a man to some special form of religion, constituting in its lowest phase that bigoted and intolerant dogmatism of priestcraft which is so indissolubly connected with the history of Christianity. Our object is to help those who are struggling for the light, and we can do this best, not by fiercely denouncing and ridiculing those doctrines which they have hitherto believed, but by showing their *relative* nature and interpreting them on deeper principles.

And so we may take one by one the difficulties which arise in the minds of those who first suspect, and finally conclude, that Christian doctrine cannot be literally and historically true ; and we may show that all these doctrines have a basis in deep and abiding principles of human nature ; that when the shell has been cracked and thrown away, the kernel will be found. The shell is the result of human sin and ignorance ; it is the encrustation of matter and form which is inevitable when the spiritual is brought down into the material. The Word must be made manifest in the Flesh, otherwise it is not seen of men ; but the Flesh is never the Word, is never the reality, though men in their ignorance fail to discriminate, and the Church has perpetuated the error, and materialized the Word into grosser and still grosser forms ; so that now when men cry for the spiritual bread of life, it has nothing to offer them but a stone.

The Church gives us no alternative but to accept or reject its dogmas. There is no inner or spiritual meaning in its teachings apart from their literal acceptation. There is no Esoteric Christianity in the Church, we must go elsewhere for it ; and it is Theosophy which now proclaims it.

So, taking this first and fundamental difficulty with regard to the origin and nature of the Bible, we do not deny, but we assert that it is a revelation ; that it is an inspiration ; that it is if you like *superhuman*, inasmuch as it comes from those who, in virtue of their position and knowledge, would be generally regarded as super-human. But the Bible as we have it now is not the original record. It has passed through many hands and many translations, and the process is inevitably a deteriorating one. The faults and errors and discrepancies are human, the result of ignorant intervention ; the underlying truth is divine, inasmuch as it deals with eternal verities.

How are we to distinguish the truth, how are we to get at these verities ? By accepting facts, knowledge, revelation, from every other source available, and interpreting the Bible by these facts, not the facts by the Bible. If we ignorantly and superstitiously suppose that the whole of revelation is contained between the covers of the Bible, and refuse to accredit—as the Church has done in all ages—anything which appears to conflict with the Scriptures, we shall never reach the truth. All that history, all that science, all that symbology and mythology can teach us, must be applied to correct and interpret the record.

And here we must notice another fact. The Bible as we now have it is a collection of a number of scattered records, selected from a great many more of a similar character. There is no reason for regarding those which have been selected as of greater value or inspiration than those which have been left out. Not only is this so, but we have in other languages, and coming down to us from nations antedating the Jewish race, similar records, dealing with the creation of the world and the relation of man to the universe, in a totally different way, though still to all appearances historically.

Now these accounts cannot be all true ; they are on the face of them quite at variance with each other.

Either the Bible is true as history—I am referring now to the account in *Genesis*—and the others false, or the Bible is false and the others true; or there is a third alternative, that they are all allegorical. Up to a certain point men may be satisfied to accept one or other of these records as historically true. There are thousands even to-day who accept literally the narrative in *Genesis*. But if we reject them as history, how shall we deal with them? Shall we throw them aside as worthless fables, belonging to a primitive and ignorant age? The answer is, No! We must call to our aid the result of literary research into ancient civilizations, customs, religions, and symbology; and by careful comparison we shall soon discover the key which we require. For there is a great mass of research and literature now available for those who really desire to get at the truth.

And when we do this we shall find that the collection of writings known as the *Bible*, constitutes but one of a number of records which are all derived from, and based upon one unifying system, known at times as the *Ancient Wisdom Religion*, or *Secret Doctrine*. We shall find that these teachings were always symbolical and mythological; that they have been given out from time to time, and from age to age, in a form appropriate to the particular nation or age for whom they were written; and that they were usually based upon some actual historical narrative, which thus gave a colour of literal truth to them. As in our childhood we demand fairy stories, and delight in fancies, so in the spiritual childhood of a man, of a nation, or a race, there is much which naturally takes the form of allegory. But these allegories are not the invention of primitive man, any more than children invent their own fairy tales. They were put forward by the divine hierarchy of *Initiates*, as the only available method of presenting truths which as yet could not be grasped in any other form.

And as it was with the early Initiates from whom all the sacred records were originally derived, so it has been with all the great teachers of whom we have historical records. Confucius and Buddha; Moses, Jesus, and Paul; one and all have had to teach in accordance with the capacity of their hearers; veiling the deeper spiritual truth in a form which was comprehensible to the people they addressed. Yet they have all indicated plainly that there was a spiritual truth underlying the form in which they taught; they have all had their *esoteric* doctrine, and their initiated disciples.

And this esoteric doctrine is the same all the world over, and in all ages; for it is the spiritual truth of man's relation to the universe, the spiritual mystery of his life and consciousness, and can only be discerned and understood by those who have risen above the illusions of time and sense, of matter and form. Let those who deny the existence of this esoteric truth explain what St. Paul means when he tells the Corinthians: " And I, brethren, could not speak unto you as unto spiritual, but as unto carnal, as unto babes in Christ. I fed you with milk, not with meat; for ye were not yet able to bear it: nay, not even now are ye able: for ye are yet carnal." (I. Cor. iii., 1.)

And it is just this *esoteric* truth, this inner spiritual meaning of the great teachers of the world, and the records they have given us, which Theosophy offers. Not by any means the whole of it, for there must still remain mystery within mystery, until the final triumph, but assuredly enough to point the way to those who are striving after a deeper knowledge, and a purer light.

And the proof that the key which Theosophy offers is the true one is its universality. The proof lies in the fact, which each one must verify for himself, that it does unify the records and teachings, which, taken in their mere outward form, appear to be contradictory and mutually destructive.

This point cannot be emphasized too strongly; it is ever the letter that killeth, but the spirit that giveth life. We have learnt nothing of our own individual life, or of the universe around us, until we have learnt to recognise the unity which underlies diversity, until we have learnt to detach the underlying spiritual principle from any mere form of doctrine, from any

mere arrangement of letters in the name of deity, from
any particular scriptural record, or conventional form
of worship. How many professing Christians are there
who can conceive of deity—using the term for the
ultimate spiritual basis of the manifested universe—
apart from the conventional name of the personal God,
Jehovah? They regard with pious horror, if not with
contempt, the "heathen" whose conception of deity is
expressed in some other arrangement of letters. To
whisper to them the name of *Brahmā* is to call up in
their minds vague notions of idol worship, strange
figures of Hindu gods, and a mysterious and superstitious worship. They send missionaries to convert
these ignorant heathen from a worship of Brahmā to a
worship of Jehovah, and the missionaries soon find out
that far from being ignorant the Brahmins are more
than a match for them on every point. However, they
send home a few samples of the four-headed Brahmā and
other "idols", and these serve to keep up the pity and
contempt—and the subscriptions. And all the time
Brahmā and Jehovah are essentially identical! Even
exoterically, in the mere external form they are identical,
Jehovah as the tetragrammaton or "four-lettered word"
I.H.V.H.; Brahmā as the four-headed god. To understand this in its deeper meaning, you must understand
the relation between the triad and the quaternary (See
diagram, page 23), as symbols of the spiritual and
the material, the eternal and the temporal, the subjective and the objective. The Brahmin will explain this
to you, the Christian will commonly deny the whole
subject.

Alas! for the illusion of forms and formulas; how
shall we teach men to escape from it? How shall we
combat that fatal disease which is the cause of all the
cruelty, intolerance and bigotry which has ever been
associated with the name of religion. There is only one
way in which it can be done—by disclosing the unifying
principle, the basis upon which all religions rest, and
from which they have all been derived. And for those
who cannot enter into the literary and critical evidences

C

of this unity, we must present a few easily understood
principles which will enable them to appreciate its
practical and moral aspect. And this is done in our
Theosophy by the doctrines of Reincarnation and
Karma. Reincarnation and Karma do not apply
merely to our individual lives, they are universal
principles. They find a reflection in our individual
lives, because they are universal principles ; for there is
nothing in man, the microcosm, that does not exist in
the universe, the macrocosm ; nor is there anything in
the universe which does not exist in man. We are
sometimes asked to prove the truth of Reincarnation
and Karma in their individual aspect by chapter and
verse from the Bible, but those who demand such proof
are those who are still in bondage to the letter, and the
least likely to grasp an underlying principle. What is
there that cannot be proved or disproved at will, by
taking mere isolated texts of Scripture ? " The Devil
can quote Scripture for his own ends ", has become a
proverb. And so although there are many isolated
texts and incidents in evidence of these doctrines as
applied to the individual, as for instance the reference
to the reincarnation of Elijah (Mat. xvii., 10) ; the
mystical application of the principle in John iii.. 3-15 ;
and the reference to Karma operating at birth in the
case of the man who was born blind (John ix., 1). In
this case Jesus is made to say that the blindness was not
the result of sin, either in the case of the man himself
before birth—for it is evident that the sin which would
cause a man to be born blind could only be accomplished
in a previous life—or of his parents ; and the rest of the
chapter is made to turn upon this incident in order to
convey deeper spiritual truths, which those who read
the mere narrative will inevitably miss. The key to
the whole chapter is contained in the last three verses :
" And Jesus said, For judgment came I into this world,
that they which see not may see ; and that they which
see may become blind. . . . . The Pharisees
said unto him, Are we also blind ? Jesus said unto them,
If ye were blind, ye would have no sin : but now ye say

we see : your sin remaineth." Thus the man who was born blind in the narrative stands for the natural spiritual blindness of those whose evolution has not yet reached that point where the " works of God " became manifest in them through the indwelling Christ principle, the " light of the world ". To this natural blindness no sin attaches, but the sin remains with those who say " We see ", yet cast out of the synagogue those whose eyes have really been opened by the divine Master. Are there no such Pharisees to-day ?

The whole chapter is a good illustration of the method which pertains all through the Bible. " The narratives of the Doctrine are its cloak. The simple look only at the garment, that is, upon the narrative of the Doctrine ; more they know not. The instructed, however, see not merely the cloak, but what the cloak covers." And it is only when you have grasped this principle, when you have understood that the genius of the Bible is not in its narrative, that you will be able to understand the value of the book, or harmonize it with natural law, and with those factors which enter into man's spiritual aspirations in all ages, and in every form of religion. And when you have been able to do this, you will see how the whole relation of man to the universe, of humanity to divinity, which the Bible discloses to those who can put aside the narrative, is based on the principles of Reincarnation and Karma ; on Reincarnation as the principle which is ever operating in the manifestation of *life*, or the constant interchange between the subjective and the objective, the alternate bringing into objectivity, and as constant disappearance into subjectivity, known to us as birth and death ; on Karma as the principle of the conservation of energy, or the co-relation of forces, operating between the subjective and the objective, applied to the universe as a whole, and to man in all his relations, physical, psychic, mental, and spiritual. For just as the whole objective universe comes into existence out of subjectivity, so does our individual life. Nothing that exists in the universe can ever cease to Be. It may change its form, or disappear altogether from our present objective plane of phenomena, but it is only the *form* which has been destroyed, and death is ever coincident with birth.

Let us now proceed to examine more in detail the Bible narrative, and the key which Theosophy offers for its interpretation. I cannot stay to point out the application of the key to the book of *Genesis*, or the other writings of the Old Testament, but must pass on to the more specific doctrines of Christianity, based upon the New Testament record ; and in doing so, I will remark upon the solution which Theosophy offers as to the supposed connection between the Old and the New Testaments in the fulfilment of prophecy.

The prophetic utterances with reference to the Messiah, and their supposed fulfilment in Jesus Christ, constitute one of the most difficult subjects in connection with Biblical criticism, as well as one of the fundamental doctrines upon which Christianity rests. If there be no connection between the Old and New Testaments in this matter, Christianity falls to the ground. The necessity for the coming of a Messiah according to Christian doctrine was owing to the " fall " of man : he was pre-ordained, prophesied, and awaited from the moment of that fall.

Now that " fall " is allegorically represented in *Genesis*. I am not speaking now to those who believe that the whole of humanity is sinful and degraded because Eve ate an apple some six thousand years ago. There is no spiritual knowledge possible for those who are so wedded to the letter, for the letter kills the spirit. But the question is : was there in the history of man's evolution, in his relation to the spiritual world, anything equivalent to a " fall"? The Esoteric Doctrine answers, yes ; and explains this fall in connection with certain well recognised cyclic laws of involution and evolution. Spiritual man " falls " every time he incarnates in physical life : for all are agreed that our present state of existence is not merely temporary, but subject to conditions which are much lower than those of a spiritual state. And so also Adam, representing generically the whole human race, "fell" from his original state of freedom and purity by eating the fruit of the tree of the knowledge of good and evil. In other words, in order that there may be evolution there must be involution. Man as a spiritual being can only become self-conscious through experience of "good and evil"; that is to say, through a descent into matter and physical life, by passage through those lower planes of cosmic life and consciousness which constitute the phenomenal world of manifestation, where everything is inseparably connected in our consciousness with its opposite; for it is this opposition or duality in all things—good and evil, light and darkness, life and death, here and there, then and now—which is the basis of all phenomena. And so when we look beneath the mere words of the allegory we find the deepest philosophical meaning; we have room for the mind to expand towards those deeper problems of life and consciousness which have occupied the profoundest thinkers in all ages, and in which the mystery of our spiritual life lies hidden.

But as man has fallen, so he must also rise; and his final triumph over evil, or Satan, or matter—for the three are synonymous—is foreshadowed in the type of the Messiah, and fully represented in the New Testament by the resurrected Christ. "For as in Adam all die, so also in Christ shall all be made alive." (I. Cor. xv., 22.) Do you suppose this refers to mere physical death? It does so apply on the lowest or physical plane of consciousness, but "as above so below", and there is a spiritual death as well as a physical; they are only synonymous inasmuch as every mystery in "heaven" is repeated on "earth"; and they are not coincident.

Spiritual man must "die", otherwise there could be no resurrection from the dead in a spiritual sense; and since spiritual man is immortal and eternal, he "dies" every time he incarnates upon this earth, for verily this world is the grave of the spirit, where it sleeps, unconscious of, or but dimly recollecting, its higher and nobler life.

And as with the individual, so with the race. As Adam is the type, so also is Christ. As the Old Testament deals with the history of man in his " fall ", foreshadowing at intervals his final redemption under the type of the Messiah, so the New Testament is the natural fulfilment of that prophecy, because it deals with the nature and conditions of this redemption under the type of Jesus Christ.

Is not that a natural and rational explanation of the nature of prophecy, and of the connection between the Old and the New Testaments ? You will see at once how it places in the background, as of quite secondary importance, all those supposed discrepancies between the actual words of a prophecy, and their literal fulfilment in the historical narrative of Jesus of Nazareth. We pass over the lowest aspect of the question, we ignore those controversial points over which such an enormous amount of learning and sophistry has been expended, and draw our inspiration from the deep philosophical and spiritual meaning of the record.

The Old Testament contains the record of man's " fall ", contains under the form of an historical allegory the secret of those vast cosmic cycles by which spirit manifests in matter, by which the divine becomes human. These cycles are portrayed in the sacred books of the East as the outbreathing and inbreathing of Brahmâ. Even modern philosophy, which as yet is but the echo of the ancient Wisdom, has given a hint at the philosophic rationale of the " fall ". According to Hegel, the " Unconscious " would never have undertaken the vast and laborious task of evolving the Universe, except in the hope of attaining self-consciousness. As above so below : our individual sentient life is the reflection of the macrocosmic principle.

And as in the Old Testament the divine becomes human, so in the New Testament the human re-becomes divine. The New Testament contains in the form of an historical allegory the conditions of man's " redemption ", that is to say, of his return to the spiritual planes of being, plus that self-consciousness, that " knowledge of good and evil ", which is the purpose of his incarnation.

The eternal law of ceaseless motion which lies at the root of cosmic evolution, finds its reflection in both small and great ; in the tiniest atom and in the most glorious sun ; in the sentient life of the lowest organism, up to man, and from man onward through all the divine hierarchies to that sum total which is unnameable.

To those who are familiar with the teachings of the *Secret Doctrine* this is readily understandable, but for the sake of those who are not I must now call your attention to a symbolism which will be found to apply to these principles under whatever form they may be given, whether in the Bible or in other ancient records.

Considering man as dual in his nature, or spiritual and material, we have as a symbol of spiritual man, a triad, represented geometrically by the triangle ; and as the symbol of material or physical man we have a quaternary, or square. I cannot stay to explain now why spiritual man is a trinity and material man a quaternary, but the fact that you find it so in every system is a significant one. Now the three and the four together make up seven, or the seven *Principles* of man as taught in Theosophy.

7		Atma	*Spirit*	The Immortal Spiritual Man
6		Buddhi	*Spiritual Soul*	or
5		Manas	*Mind*	Divine Ego.
4		Kama	*Animal Soul*	
3		Prana	*Vitality*	The Mortal Physical Man
2		Astral	*Double*	or
1		Physical	*Body*	Temporary Personality.

The three higher principles constitute the immortal, divine, spiritual man ; or the individuality, the *Ego sum*. The four lower belong to the temporary personality of physical, material man.

At death, the four lower principles disappear, or disintegrate into their natural elements on the four planes to which they belong, while the consciousness of the man that was is withdrawn into the higher triad. At rebirth, or reincarnation, this is outbreathed again, clothes itself in the elements of the four lower planes, or " matter ", and becomes again a human being for the purpose of a new cycle of experience. Thus you will see that at every birth into this world, or at every re-incarnation, there is relatively a " fall", though absolutely it is a rise, on account of the experience gained. Now we see this great law of cyclic motion, or of outbreathing and inbreathing, in operation in every form of manifestation in the universe, taking the form of a law of periodicity, or of alternate subjectivity and objectivity ; smaller cycles operating within larger ones in ever-increasing magnitude, to infinity. And just as individual man in his repeated manifestations or incarnations follows this law, so does the whole of humanity in its aggregate of evolution upon this earth, during *its* period of manifestation ; and this descent into matter constitutes the allegory of the Book of Genesis, and is continued under other symbols in other books of the Old Testament.

But man has to win his way back to his original free-dom. Having entered " matter " he must fight and overcome it. The necessity for reincarnation is con-ditioned by his not having as yet accomplished the object for which the original impulse to incarnation was given. When that object is accomplished, man rises as the conqueror over death—because the conqueror over the necessity of rebirth—as the glorified *Christos*, the perfected Adept, or full Initiate. " Then shall come to pass the saying that is written, Death is swallowed up in victory." (I. Cor. xv., 54.) And it is this victory, this conquest, and the conditions under which it must be obtained, which is portrayed in the New Testament.

I think I have said enough now to show the connec-tion between the Old and New Testaments, and to give you the clue to their interpretation ; for it is impossible to do more than give the clue to those whose minds are open to the underlying mysteries; and I must now pass on to deal more specifically with some of the doctrines based on the New Testament record.

The first thing which is necessary in doing this is to dispose of the historical difficulty. There are many who will accept an allegorical Adam as a type of humanity, who will not accept an allegorical and typical Christ. But the one without the other is an impossibility, as indeed is plainly seen in the writings of St. Paul. "As we have borne the image of the earthy, we shall also bear the image of the heavenly." (II. Cor. xv., 49.) There is no choice between the literal personal and historical character of both, and the doctrines of the fall and atonement as taught by the Church, or the allegorical and typical character of the one as of the other. They are indissolubly connected, and whatever key is used for the one must be used for the other.

But the difficulty is not so great as it appears, and admits of a very simple solution. Just as in the Old Testament we have the historical Jewish race, into whose history is cunningly woven the thread of the mystical allegory of man's evolution, so in the New Testament we have the historical Jesus, into whose life and teachings is woven the mystical truths of the nature of the divine man. There cannot be an historical *Christ*, any more than an historical Adam; for every man is Adam, and every man will become *Christos*, or "anointed". But we have an actual historical *Jesus*, and everyone i at liberty to believe what he likes as to that historical character being already *Christos*, the perfect man, or Initiate.

Thus we may reconcile in whatever way we please, from literary and critical evidences, the difficulties which arise in the Gospel narratives respecting the personality of Jesus of Nazareth, without interfering in the slightest degree with the divine nature and mystery of the *Christ*.

It will be seen at once how this disposes of the importance of those difficulties over which so much controversy has been wasted, during centuries of ecclesiastical teaching, and which still rages in the present day. The "divinity of Christ" has been the great dogma of the Church, and at the same time the great stumbling-block of rational thought, simply because the *blind* was so complete—or rather because the early Church authorities were so successful in destroying the clue, so that the derivation of their doctrines from the Gnostic and Egyptian *Mysteries* could not be traced—that the personal *Jesus* became absolutely identified with the typical *Christ*.

But the truth cannot be withheld from the world much longer. Literary and historical research, and comparative symbology and mythology, is gradually disclosing the fraud which has been imposed upon the world for centuries. The truth will soon be clearly and undeniably demonstrated, and while ecclesiastical Christianity may remain as a remnant of superstition, the truth as it is in Christ will shine forth as the spiritual light upon the inmost mystery of man's nature.

The divinity of Christ is as certain as the humanity of Adam. The one completes the other. If Christ was not divine, then is humanity not divine; and there is no salvation possible for it. If humanity is not divine, then there could have been no Christ, and all men's spiritual aspirations are empty dreams.

The doctrine of the divine incarnation was taught in all the Ancient Mysteries. We have the story, incident by incident, almost word for word as in the Gospels, in many other so-called *heathen* systems. In the Egyptian, as Horus, the son of Osiris and Isis, we have the same typical Messiah in connection with a solar or astronomical glyph. So also with Krishna, the son of Vishnu and Lakshmi, we have so near an approach to the Gospel narrative, that it has been the greatest puzzle, and has led to the most flagrant literary dishonesty, to endeavour to account for the narratives, without deriving the one from the other. But all these difficulties vanish the moment we understand the real nature of the divine incarnation, and its connection with natural evolution and universal laws.

And observe further how this is the bridge which

spans the gulf between science and religion. We are
often told that there can be no conflict between true
science and true religion; yet nothing is more notorious
than the open conflict between the representatives of
the one and of the other. The Church has ever been
the deadliest enemy of scientific discovery, and to-day,
if she had the power, she would burn its votaries as she
did of old. But there can be no conflict with the
religion we now advance, based upon the relation of
man to the universe, instead of upon an anthropomorphic
God. The scientific materialist may doubt our conclusions, but we have no quarrel with the facts he brings
to light. If his special line of research blinds him to
higher spiritual possibilities, so much the worse for him;
but we welcome as so much gain all that he can teach
us as to nature's methods of working. And so also in
other departments of research, all that is brought to
light is clear gain to us. There is no longer any fear
lest our favourite dogmas should be overturned, lest the
foundations of our faith should crumble to dust before
the advancing tide of knowledge. We welcome knowledge in every shape and form, for in knowledge there is
freedom, but in ignorance is superstition, fear, cruelty,
and death.

Let us now turn for a moment to the symbol of the
cross, which is supposed to be so pre-eminently origi-
nated by, and associated with, Christian doctrine. It
is a matter of secondary importance to us whether the
personal Jesus was or was not crucified in the manner
described; as to whether he did or did not rise from the
grave, and appear afterwards to his disciples. The
speculations, and arguments, and physical probability
or improbability of this event may be left to those who
still cling to the idea of a carnalised personal *Christ*.
Supposing for a moment that it did happen as narrated,
it by no means follows that the dogmas built thereon
are true; but whether it did or did not happen, does
not interfere with the spiritual meaning and significance.
Here again the Church is a blind leader of the blind.
We must go further and deeper, we must study symbology,

mythology, and astronomy even, before we can understand how the symbol of the cross came to be associated
with spiritual man, as the *Christos*. In selecting and
editing the books of the New Testament as we now
have them, the Church took care to obliterate all traces
which would disclose the real source and meaning of
this symbol. They did more. The hordes of fanatical
Christians searched for and ruthlessly destroyed all the
ancient manuscripts, sculptures, hieroglyphs, and other
records which bore testimony to its use prior to the
Christian era. Some of the hieroglyphs, cut into the
hard stone of the Egyptian rock temples, which they
could not deface, they plastered over with stucco, thus
taking the very best precautions to preserve the writing
clear and well-defined for our use. But the evidences
are now too numerous to be denied, that the cross has
been a universal symbol in all ages. What did it
mean ?

The cross in its simplest form, as +, is the glyph for
the quaternary or square, representing as we have
already seen the four lower planes of consciousness, or
more simply, *matter*. Astronomically also, in conjunc-
tion with the circle, as ⊕ it is the symbol for the
earth. It is also known as the " mundane cross ", and
s expressed in various forms in different systems, as the
" swastica " ⌐⌐, the "ansated cross" ⸸, the "tau" T, &c.
On our three dimensional plane the square becomes
the cube, and the cube unfolded again displays the cross.

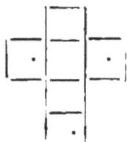

The two members counted separately give
us 3 and 4, or together 7; while the addi-
tion of the three nail marks gives us the
suggestion of the triangle, or the divine
man crucified on the cross of matter.

We shall thus see, in accordance with
what has already been explained, that
every incarnation of the divine spirit, whether individually or collectively, constitutes of necessity a crucifixion. The incarnated Christ must needs be crucified.
It is simply the summing up in one glyph, in one
allegory, of the whole mystery, the consummation in

one figurative emblem of the whole drama of human existence. And as he must needs be crucified, must needs descend into matter, so he must needs resurrect, and re-ascend to claim his spiritual birthright. " If Christ hath not been raised, then is our preaching vain." (I Cor. xv., 14.)

There are other applications and interpretations of this symbol, too numerous and complicated to enter into here. Each of these symbols has seven meanings, corresponding to the seven planes of consciousness through which the man passes, or in which he lives. In its lowest signification the cross is a purely physiological symbol, and as such led to its identification with phallic worship.

The astronomical key, the connection of the twelve tribes of Israel and the twelve apostles with the twelve signs of the zodiac, and of the Messiah, in the various events and characteristics of his history, with the yearly passage of the sun through these twelve signs, is full of interest and significance. Some writers having discovered this astronomical key in connection with the Messiah, and its equal application to other mythical characters, more particularly to Osiris and Horus, in the Egyptian system, have supposed that this was the real source and origin of the Christian Mythos, and the only explanation of which it is capable. The *Secret Doctrine*, however, draws aside the veil from some of the other interpretations, gives the clue to other of the seven keys, and thereby raises it once more from the physical and material into the psychic and spiritual.

The symbolism of the zodiac was, and still is, one of the greatest secrets of the *Mysteries*. It is the type of that great law, which, operating universally in periodic cycles, brings about that change which we call *evolution*. Working eternally through the material basis of the universe, through " root substance", it brings to life and brings to death, and brings to life again. Atoms and worlds, organic life in every phase, from tiniest cell, from the first germs of sentient life onward through all its grades, from the first dawn of individual con-

sciousness, through plant and animal, to men and gods :
this great law holds its sway. Cycle within cycle in
ever-widening magnitude, until the mind of man is lost
in contemplation of the infinite ; and yet, through all
and in all such unity and harmony that could we but
see and understand, we should find at every mathematical
point in space—the whole universe. And thus one
type stands for all, one symbology is of universal application ; and were we wise as those ancient sages who
gave to the world that symbology, of which we have now
but the broken fragments, we should indeed be able to
read man's destiny in the stars.

We must now turn our attention for a few moments
to the Christian doctrine of the Atonement, or as it
ought more properly to be called, the at-one-ment. I
am not supposing now that any of my hearers are
believers in the dogma that the actual sufferings of a
physical Christ were the propitiation of an angry God.
One would think that the actual sufferings of humanity
itself since the " fall " was propitiation enough to satisfy
any God with a sense of justice at least equal to our
own. But be that as it may, I must now show that this
doctrine, grossly as it has been materialized, can still
be reconstructed on esoteric lines.

Turn to our diagram of the seven principles of man.
(Page 23.) We have spiritual or divine man as a
trinity, corresponding to the supreme divine trinity which
is found in every ancient system, and from which the
Christian trinity was derived, and ultimately promul-
gated as a dogma when Athanasius triumphed over
Arius. Now in this trinity of Atma-Buddhi-Manas,
Atma corresponds to the "Father" and "Manas" to
the "Son". Manas is always spoken of as the incar-
nating Ego, that which is the informing principle of our
successive re-births upon earth. This statement however is only partial in its application. The mystery of
the trinity, the three in one and the one in three, is
repeated on earth. Atma-Buddhi-Manas are not three
but one, yet viewed *relatively*, or in their individual
capacity, they have to be treated as separate entities.

A very familiar analogy will illustrate this, and indeed, under the form of "divine ideation," lies at the root of this metaphysical trinity. Wherever you have a *thinker*, you must also have a *thought* and a *thing thought of.* You cannot separate these three, the one cannot exist without the other, yet each of these three principles may be individualized and treated separately. In other words, wherever there is the action of conscious intelligence, whether of God or man, there must be a trinity. Now just as *Manas* is an individualized aspect of *Atma*—the seventh or highest, the one universal principle, or synthesis of all the others—being so to speak a ray or Mahat, or universal mind, so our personal consciousness, the thinking principle of the lower quaternary—or in short, ourselves—is but an individualized aspect, or ray of Manas. In other words, Manas, the divine Ego, is not comprised in the personality, but overshadows and guides it. We have already seen that in doing this it is symbolically crucified on the cross of matter, for it attaches to itself and becomes responsible for all the deeds of the personality, good or evil. Thus it is truly the sacrificial victim, suffering for our transgressions, for the sins of humanity.

And observe how the only hope of salvation for the personality—for ourselves—the only way in which we can escape from the evil of matter, from the "great illusion", the "great deceiver"—or in short the *Devil*— the only way in which we can reach that perfection of our humanity which is typified in Christ : is by union with our *Alter Ego*, our *Higher Self ;* or by means of that indwelling Christ which Paul preached. If we persistently turn from the light, if we refuse to follow the promptings of our conscience, and choose the path of evil, we weaken more and more the bond which connects the higher with the lower, until at last perchance the link is snapped, and there is no longer any possibility of salvation. This is the "sin against the Holy Ghost".

Observe how this is taught all through St. John's Gospel. "I am the way, and the truth, and the life : no one cometh unto the Father, but through Me"

(John xiv., 6). For as Manas is one with Atma, we can only reach the latter, or the " Father " through union with Manas. And this is something which must take place here and now, by our own conscious efforts, and not as a miraculous dispensation of "providence ". At death all that is *spiritual* in our character becomes indrawn, so to speak, by the overshadowing Ego. All that belongs to the four lower principles is dissolved and disintegrated, or awaits us as *Karma* for our next rebirth, while the personal consciousness realises in full all its spiritual aspirations in a state of bliss or " Heaven ". But this is only possible to the extent to which each individual has cherished and intensified those aspirations. Each one goes to his appointed place, or rather state. The judgment book is opened, the imperishable record of every thought and deed, traced in the great law of cause and effect, will assign to each his appropriate reward, and in rebirth his appropriate penalty. Let none hope to escape the law of absolute justice.

> " It seeth everywhere and marketh all :
>   Do right—it recompenseth ! do one wrong—
>   The equal retribution must be made,
>   Though DHARMA tarry long.
>
> It knows no wrath nor pardon ; utter true
>   Its measures mete, its faultless balance weighs ;
>   Times are as nought, to-morrow it will judge.
>   Or after many days."

And if we would escape rebirth, if we would triumph over death and the cross, we can only do so by this perfect union with our Higher Self, with the Christ within us. And just as the accomplishment of this individually is the complete union of the personality with the higher triad, so for the race collectively it is the return of that cycle when spirit will once more triumph over matter, typified in the New Testament as the "second coming of Christ." And then the " Son " having accomplished his work, becomes once more one with the " Father ". This is the *Pralaya*, or "inbreathing of Brahmâ", in Eastern phraseology ; while St.

Paul expresses it by saying: "And when all things have been subjected unto him, then shall the Son also himself be subjected to him that did subject all things unto him, that God may be all in all" (I. Cor., xv., 28).

Read the mystical Gospel of St. John in the light of this interpretation, and see what a flood of light it throws upon the constant references to the relationship between the "Father" and the "Son", personified in Jesus. The "Father" of John's Gospel never was and never can be the personal tribal God of the Israelites—Jehovah; although the Church has fathered him upon Christendom. The sayings and claims of Jesus are absurd when personified, but are pregnant with meaning, and the deepest truth when applied to universal principles. "As the living Father sent me, and I live because of the Father; so he that eateth me, he also shall live because of me. This is the bread which came down from heaven: not as the fathers did eat, and died: he that eateth this bread shall live for ever". (John vi. 57.) This passage bears on the face of it its mystical and figurative character. Yet because the Church has materialized it, and succeeded in imposing upon the world a personal *Christ*, it has given rise to some of the grossest forms of superstitious ritual.

The Pharisees of old were the representatives of all that was narrow, formal, mechanical, and material in religion. They practised a ritual from which the spirit had fled, of which the key had been lost; they made clean the outside of the vessel, but inwardly it was full of extortion and wickedness. And so it was the Pharisees who cried out, "Crucify him! Crucify him!" Do you suppose that was merely an historical event, or rather that it stood as the type of what happens in all ages, when the truth is sacrificed at the hands of formalism and bigotry. The crucifixion as we have already seen, stands for the descent of spirit into matter, in whatever aspect we may regard it; whether definitely and individually in our own nature, or in a more abstract way as the bringing into objectivity,

D

the giving shape and form, or the representation on the limited and conditioned plane of materiality, of universal spiritual principles. So, whenever we endeavour to give these spiritual mysteries a definite shape and form, to confine them within the limits of some system, of some cut and dried formula, of some dogma and creed, we crucify the divine on the cross of matter.

And as it was with the Pharisees, so it is with the church to-day. It daily and hourly cries out: "Crucify him! Crucify him!" In every promulgation of its dogmas; in every frantic effort which it makes to stay the advancing tide of knowledge, and keep back the truth from mankind; in every anathema it utters against those who have awakened to a sense of the deeper mysteries of their being, and seeking in vain for any light in christian teachings have turned elsewhere : the Church crucifies the Son of God afresh, and puts him to an open shame.

We do not deny or destroy christian doctrine; we affirm and re-establish it. It is the church which destroys it by making it limited and conditioned ; refusing to recognise its elasticity and application to natural laws and universal principles. All that belongs to the world of form and formulas is subject to change, decay, death. There can be no change in TRUTH; yet nothing is more palpable than the ever-fluctuating value or what is termed—*orthodoxy*. Nothing is of less value to-day than the teachings of the church in its practical influence on the conduct and social relations of the nation. The vast majority of thinkers are alienated from the church, the masses are scarcely touched by its influence. Those who profess, do not practice ; they quietly ignore everything in the teachings of Jesus which would interfere with their social affairs. All that affects our social relationships is decided on grounds of expediency which have no special basis in Christian doctrine. The Church itself has decided that it shall be so. What it teaches has reference to a future life, to a future spiritual state, not to the eternal spiritual *present*. It has no ethical standard which is not found

elsewhere, for on those very points where the ethics of
Jesus are in advance of the common morals of expediency, it tacitly admits, and even expressly declares,
that they are *impracticable*. If one tithe of professing
christians believed all that they profess, there would
be no " submerged tenth."

We have no quarrel with the sincere and devout
religionist, with those who are striving to the best of
their ability, with the light they have, to live up to
their ideal. There are hundreds of thousands who
cannot in the nature of the case enter into the esoteric
teachings. The truth must be presented to them in
some familiar and understandable form, otherwise it is
a dead letter, and a sealed book. To many, the personal
Saviour is a living reality, because they have made it
such by daily and hourly dwelling upon the ideal. To
ruthlessly destroy that ideal, without substituting an
equivalent, might lead to untold evil. Let us deal
gently and carefully with such.

Nor is there any need to destroy that ideal which is
so dear to many sincere christians. The personal
attachment to the life and character of Jesus of Nazareth
may still remain in all degrees and forms. It even
becomes greater and stronger when we understand the
true nature of his divinity, and the true nature of his
humanity. Jesus Christ is both human and divine,
because we are such.

Understand this matter well—*Jesus* is the personal
historical character, *Christ* is the *type*, which has been
grafted upon and associated with that character. *Christ*,
the " second Adam", could no more be historical than
the " first Adam " ; and those who have accepted the
mythical and allegorical character of the one, have no
choice but to do so for the other. Both are types of
humanity. " The first man is of the earth, earthy : the
second man is of heaven. As is the earthy, such are
they also that are earthy ; and as is the heavenly, such
are they also that are heavenly. *And as we have borne
the image of the earthy, we shall also bear the image of the
heavenly* ". (I Cor. xv. 47.)

There always has been and must be an exoteric and an esoteric; a religion for the masses, an initiation for the few. But when we see the blind leading the blind we are bound to step in. Even as Jesus denounced the Scribes and Pharisees of his time, so we are bound to denounce the formalism and bigotry of to-day. The Church has no esoteric doctrine, no initiated priesthood. To-day the priest nominates himself; his qualifications are for the most part social or sermonizing. Read the fifth chapter of the Epistle to the Hebrews, as to the connection between Christ and Melchizedek as the type of the high priest, of whom Paul says : " We have many things to say, and *hard of interpretation*, seeing ye are become dull of hearing. For when by reason of the time ye ought to be teachers, ye have need again that someone teach you the rudiments of the first principles of the oracles of God, and are become such as have need of milk, and not of solid food." (Heb. v., 11.) And so history repeats itself.

But those who would understand that "wisdom hidden in a mystery," which Paul preached, and which may still be discerned like a thread of gold running through his Epistles, sadly as they have been tampered with, must lay aside the "weak and beggarly elements" which hold men in bondage to the letter. And it is only when you have done this that you will know what is that "glorious liberty of the gospel of Christ," which Paul preached. " Ye observe days, and months, and seasons, and years ", he says : " I am afraid of you lest by any means I have bestowed labour upon you in vain." (Gal. iv., 10.) It is only when we can say with Paul, " I have been crucified with Christ; yet I live; and yet no longer I, but Christ liveth in me" (Gal. ii., 20), that we can lay claim to be either Christians or Theosophists. Paul meant just what Theosophists mean when they speak of union with their *Higher Self*.

" O foolish Galatians "—he says again—" Who did bewitch you before whose eyes Jesus Christ was openly set forth crucified ; " that is to say : to whom he had openly taught the knowledge of the mystic Christ, which had been kept a profound secret hitherto by the initiated Gnostics; for he adds : " Are ye so foolish ? having begun in the spirit, do ye now make an end in the flesh "? ; that is to say, having begun with the highest or spiritual signification, do ye now return to the outward worship of a carnal Christ ? Nor is it difficult to trace the connection between these words and the relation of Paul's teachings to those of Peter and the other apostles who founded the Church of Rome. Paul was an Initiate and a Gnostic. Just as St. John's Gospel is Gnostic, so are St. Paul's Epistles; and in spite of the interpolations and emendations which were made by the Church Fathers before they would allow them to be placed in the Canon, the fact cannot be disguised when once the clue is found. It was Peter, and those who with him, as apostles of the " circumcision ", preached a personal and carnal Christ, against whom Paul warned the Galatians. The subject is too large to deal with here, but it is necessary to give this hint in order that the question of Christian doctrine, derived from the authority of the church may be understood.

I have thus traversed briefly the whole ground of Biblical narrative in its connection with Christian doctrine. I have shown how every doctrine—inspiration and prophecy, the fall and the redemption, the crucifixion and the resurrection, the divinity of Christ and the atonement—are one and all susceptible of an esoteric interpretation. How these doctrines are based upon earlier teachings, known as the *Mysteries* or *Gnosis*, but were perverted and obscured by the Church, until finally the key was lost, and the Church, gaining the temporal power it coveted, imposed upon the world those dogmas which have ever been synonymous with all that is most opposed to the teachings of Jesus of Nazareth, and Paul the Apostle.

All that I have been able to do however is to point out the landmarks, to give the clue to the complicated and intricate question of Biblical history and authority. To those who are familiar with the endless controversies on the subject, with the frantic efforts which are made to reconcile legend with history, and the supernatural element with the known laws and facts of nature, this interpretation may come like cool and refreshing waters in a parched and arid desert. If they will follow up the clue they will find that the difficulties are but mirage—illusion. They will rise to a high and serene level of thought where such contentions cannot affect them. They will "shun foolish questionings, and genealogies, and strifes, and fightings about the law; for they are unprofitable and vain." And Paul adds to this a piece of advice which Theosophists would do well to remember: "A man that is factious after a first and second admonition—avoid." (Titus 3, 9.) It is impossible to teach the underlying spiritual truth to those who are still in bondage to the law, to those who have not yet cast aside the material form, but can rise to no higher ideal than that of a material heaven of endless enjoyment, and an equally material hell of endless torment.

It is time that the Christian world should lay aside the spell which has been so long cast over it. It is time that all thinking men should awake to the spiritual realities which constitute the ever-present NOW. And it is the work of Theosophy to lead the way in this spiritual revival; to free mankind from ignorance, superstition, sin, and death. Would that it might ring through the world like a trumpet-call—"AWAKE THOU THAT SLEEPEST, AND ARISE FROM THE DEAD, AND CHRIST SHALL SHINE UPON THEE."

THE THEOSOPHICAL SOCIETY.

THE Theosophical Society was formed at New York, November 17th, 1875. Its founders believed that the best interests of Religion and Science would be promoted by the revival of Sanskrit, Pali, Zend, and other ancient literature, in which the Sages had preserved for the use of mankind truths of the highest value respecting man and nature. A Society of an absolutely unsectarian character, whose work should be amicably prosecuted by the learned of all races, in a spirit of unselfish devotion to the research of truth, and with the purpose of disseminating it impartially, seemed likely to do much to check materialism and strengthen the waning spirit of true Religion, Science, and Philosophy. The simplest expression of the objects of the Society is the following :—

FIRST.—*To form the nucleus of a Universal Brotherhood of Humanity, without distinction of race, creed, sex, caste, or colour.*

SECOND.—*To promote the study of Aryan and other Eastern literatures, religions, philosophies, and sciences, and to demonstrate their importance to Humanity.*

THIRD.—*To investigate unexplained laws of nature and the psychical powers latent in man.*

The Theosophical Society is not connected with any creed or party. Its members are united by the bond of a common ideal—Brotherhood ; by a common rule of conduct—the attempt to realize that ideal ; and by a common study—that set forth in the second and third " Objects " stated above. The acceptance of these latter, however, is optional with members.

Those who join the Society are asked to part with no religious or other beliefs, consistent with a respect for, and toleration of the beliefs of other members. Few persons are without a preference for some form of creed or doctrine, not accepted by others, who are, intellectually and morally, their equals. But the motto of the Theosophical Society, "There is no religion higher than Truth," forbids all bigotry or exclusiveness, by holding up as the goal of effort something which lies above and beyond all systems, whether of philosophy, religion, or science—which admit of any doubt or question. Thus there are in its ranks, and coöperating in its work, followers of the most divergent schools of thought—Christians, Buddhists, Hindûs, Parsees, Mahommedans, Freethinkers, etc.

The promoters of the Society's objects do not even dream of being able to establish upon earth during their time an actual Brotherhood of peoples and governments. But what they do hope and mean to achieve is to induce a large body of the more reasonable and better educated persons of all races and religious groups extant, to accept and put into practice the theory that by mutual help and a generous tolerance of each other's pre-conceptions, mankind will be largely benefited and the chances of discovering hidden truth immensely increased. The policy they advocate is that of benevolent reciprocity—the Golden Rule of "doing as one would be done by," which was preached by most of the great Sages of old, and has been the watchword of true philanthropists in all epochs. They go on sowing this seed, leaving it to germinate in the fulness of time and to ultimately bear a rich harvest for the coming generations.

The Society, then, represents not any one creed, but all creeds; not one, but every branch of science. It is the opponent of bigotry, superstition. credulity, and dogmatism wherever found or by whomsoever taught. So, also, it is the opponent of vice in every form and of all that tends to feed or propagate it. It expects every one who becomes a member to avoid doing what will be likely to throw discredit upon the Society and dishonour his fellow-members. While it does not look for saint-like perfection in applicants for membership, it does hope, by holding up to them the ideal of a nobler Humanity, to make them ashamed of their vices and eager to extirpate them.

As regards the possibility of acquiring spiritual knowledge and powers, it is enough to remark here that we learn from a study of the literature of the past that the Ancients gained great psychical powers and a deep insight into Nature's secrets, and working by the rules they laid down, modern experience confirms many of their claims.

THEOSOPHY.

The mystical philosophy which gives its name to the Society, and is vaguely known under the general title " Theosophy ", is put forward by certain members as at once a result of and an incentive to that particular line of study described in " Objects " 2 and 3. They believe that the doctrines, or leading ideas, of Theosophy, both Eastern and Western, are especially worthy of attention at the present time, as suggesting the probable solution of many of the most vexed religious, social, and scientific questions of the day. An extensive literature has sprung up in connection with the Theosophical movement, in which many of these ideas are explained and discussed.

It must be borne in mind, however, that these doctrines are not advanced as dogmas, but merely as reasonable hypotheses throwing light upon many phases and conditions of life which otherwise appear incomprehensible or inconsistent. The Theosophical Society aims at assisting its members by the spread of literature, and by all other methods within its power, in their search after Truth. But the Theosophical Society itself formulates no creed, and is not bound down to any doctrines. It places no restriction upon its members beyond that of loyalty to its one fundamental principle of thought and action— Universal Brotherhood ; nor is it as a society account-

able for the opinions expressed by any of its members.
It may, however, be stated that the majority of the
members, as individuals, believe that the realization of
this first object of the Theosophical Society can best be
attained by a thorough grasp of the principles of
Theosophy, which, in their opinion, place Universal
Brotherhood on a scientific and logical basis.

THE EUROPEAN SECTION OF THE THEOSOPHICAL SOCIETY.

The Theosophical Society has many branches scattered
over the world, and in America as well as in India,
enough already to make it possible for a Theosophist
to find in almost every large city a group of brother
Theosophists to welcome him.

The Lodges and Unattached Members in Europe
form the European Section of the Society. This
Section has its Headquarters at 19, Avenue Road,
Regent's Park, London, N.W., where inquirers can
obtain all information. Inquirers and members at a
distance are assisted by being placed in correspondence
with other members of the Society.

All inquiries and correspondence should be addressed
to:

THE GENERAL SECRETARY,
19, Avenue Road,
Regent's Park,
London, N.W.

To assist students of Theosophy, the following list of
books has been drawn up for their guidance, so as to
form a graduated course of reading on the subject:

SCIENTIFIC AND PHILOSOPHICAL. £ s. d.

The Key to Theosophy, by H. P. Blavatsky   0 6 0
Esoteric Buddhism, by A. P. Sinnett   -   0 4 0

Reincarnation, by E. D. Walker - -	o	3	6
The Purpose of Theosophy, by Mrs. A. P. Sinnett - - - - -	o	3	6
Isis Unveiled (2 vols.), by H. P. Blavatsky -	2	2	o
Echoes from the Orient, by Wm. Q. Judge -	o	3	o
The Secret Doctrine (2 vols.), by H. P. Blavatsky - - - -	2	2	o

MYSTICAL AND METAPHYSICAL.

The Voice of the Silence, by H. P. Blavatsky	o	2	6
The Bhagavad-Gita - - -	o	4	6
Patanjali's Yoga Sutras - - -	o	3	6

The following low-priced pamphlets are also recommended :

Wilkesbarre Letters on Theosophy - -	6d.
Epitome of Theosophical Teachings - -	3d.
The Higher Science - - - -	2d.
The Old Wisdom-Religion - - -	6d
Theosophy and its Evidences - -	3d.

May be obtained from the THEOSOPHICAL PUBLISHING SOCIETY, 7, Duke Street, Adelphi, London, W.C.

THEOSOPHICAL SIFTINGS.

ANNUAL SUBSCRIPTION 5/-.

(The Fourth Year commenced March 1891).

A series of 18 deeply interesting pamphlets on Theosophy, Mysticism and Occultism are issued every year and are sent post free to subscribers as they appear.

Subscribers to the Siftings have the use of the T.P.S. Library, paying 2d. per week for the loan of books. Carriage extra. Send stamp for Library Catalogue.

THE THEOSOPHICAL PUBLISHING SOCIETY,
7, Duke Street, Adelphi, London, W.C.

www.ingramcontent.com/pod-product-compliance
Lightning Source LLC
Chambersburg PA
CBHW021440090426
42739CB00009B/1570